THE
NEW
SORROW
IS
LESS
THAN
THE
OLD
SORROW

THE
NEW
SORROW
IS
LESS
THAN
THE
OLD
SORROW

JENNY DRAI

Black
Lawrence
Press

Black
Lawrence
Press

www.blacklawrence.com

Executive Editor: Diane Goettel
Chapbook Editor: Kit Frick
Cover Design: Angela Leroux-Lindsey and Amy Freels
Book Design: Amy Freels

Published 2015 by Black Lawrence Press.
Printed in the United States.

TIMELINE (NOTES):

1772: Goethe at Wetzlar meets, falls in love with engaged Charlotte Buff, and in his despair considers suicide; concurrent suicide of Jerusalem, a man in love with a married woman.

1774: Publication of *The Sorrows of Young Werther,* an epistolary novel about a young man who commits suicide over his despair at being in love with an engaged woman (Lotte).

Thereafter: "Werther-Fieber" (Werther-Fever) takes Germany by storm; Sturm und Drang, a literary movement that countered the rational empiricism of the Enlightenment takes hold; literary superstardom for Goethe; spin-offs; alternative endings; commercialism of Werther (i.e. Eau de Werther and other products) and so on. Goethe becomes frustrated by so much attention on one specific early piece. Later, he comes to turn away from his early work and, with Schiller, promotes Weimar Classicism.

TIMELINE (AUTOBIOGRAPHY):

1997–1999: A few post-collegiate years in Munich. Working as au pair, cleaning apartments for extra money. Reading *The Sorrows of*

Young Werther for the first time, every time. Falling in love with a flesh-and-blood young man in a foreign language, another country.

Thereafter: Leaving, continuing, leaving, returning. Leaving.

NOTES:

he (Werther) spoke to his own limbs and chose to cast off a
subject of disabled nearness. couldn't embrace her, as if,
peering through water, he had jimmied himself into a
preoccupation cage. I told you to read the last parts. has
changed nothing. still I turn the next blank page. an imploded
wave, those copycat suicides. a little ruby on white pillows.
here I have had a little too much drink. here I have him saved.
the only way to hold is as to break.

this eye is a lackey and very blue. Goethe in old age, running away from the dreary gray book. the other writer who tricked the story and filled the pistol with chicken blood. so that Werther might live. in old age, Goethe despised his own emotion. this wound is rub-salt, very full of noise. someone, somewhere, worships at a shrine. memory is full of embarrassment and embarrassment. young G., apprenticed to the law, in love with C.B., Charlotte Buff, one version of nude. she is a story conflated with one story, her love for Kestner. no surprise for outcome.

many, many times I answer to the succinct question *how often have you?* the rational subjectively. of all lungs that inhale antecedent. a number of options loiter on counters. sweet, time-bruised plums. not decisions but placeholders. if enough, is not enough, written-out fog, carefully plucked. yes. plucked fog. I dare you. throw water against your heart as if that dragnet of emotions were a cliff. then master it.

take care, body. weight cast with value is composed of those who envy weight and those who could despise it. Goethe may need assurances, more light, the science of colors. how the visitors come but have only read the one text, written at the age of twenty-four. to be known. passion-trigger-passion. someone, somewhere, worships in a grotto at a shrine to suicide. the pain of. the remittance of. love. which is not to say it was not *smiled upon*. Charlotte Buff, you rue the day. a man named Jerusalem takes his own life. he is a *true-life example* of danger. eating a tongue swallowing a heart. undefeated, he couldn't quite attempt, but did G. ever contemplate. *ever* not a question but an answer.

Werther is the take-up, the glint-black weapon in this illumination, when I closed you. saying *near enough* or something like yellow margarine smeared across kernels of toast, the victorious whole grains. very rational to ingest, also, a decision. the necessity of counterparts. like opening up a velvet case to stare at ghosts. temples. expediency. all right. one ought to dip one's hand in the water, grasping not mere stones, the trinkets of current. nor baubles cast off from shores with flighty motions. rather, the real *stuff*. every discernable tangent. but still, not to be so ruled, solely, this red map.

eat arsenic. get a black tongue. pistol equals dime-sized ruby. a keen love that hurts and breaks bones. you just get all crushed feeling. noose-neck chafe, frigid river chilling still the bones. youth is a very unrequited eyesore. *I able it* the text belies the later, older man. *once I was so wounded I made a fresh wound.* in old age Goethe could not stomach this purgative and slightly rued the day. no one comes to talk to him about *Elective Affinities. I able love in a parlor that must not be returned.* of course, that was a very different book. people gave in.

could bend ankles away from incongruous places. that is, or,
that is not. a lark really, *or a sparrow,* to place those fingers *so,*
just *so* on the lacy graveclothes. if you insist upon this route,
you will lose the house of staircases. but deeply. come. taste.
these slowly sloping cadences of stone. saved, rescued,
rejuvenated, resuscitated. in another place, ending at the not-
end. please. walk through short hallways. imitate the clamor
of doors opening swiftly.

everybody *once*.

Autobiography

LIST OF FOREIGN WORDS (in order of appearance):

bitte Fenster putzen:	clean the windows, please
die Bäckerei:	the bakery
Tabak:	tobacco
Stimme:	voice
alte Dame:	old lady
moya dryzuuya, kak tebya:	my friend, how are you
DMs:	Deutschmarks
nyet kracuuvuuya:	not beautiful
lieben:	to love
Kastanienbäume:	chestnut trees
das Treppenhaus:	the inner stairwell
	(as in an apartment house)
Liebe:	love

excuse moi, Monsieur, je ne parl paux ... parlez vouz?

excuse me, Sir, I don't speak ... do you speak?

bunte:	colorful
ich komme:	I am coming
Schirre:	scissors
braun-äugig:	brown-eyed
zurück:	back (the preposition,
	not the noun)
Alltag:	everyday
Semmeln ...	breakfast rolls ...

AUTOBIOGRAPHY:

I.

continuously with air the body climbs a staircase. I
intend to buy you supper, coin denting the hand. at
some shriveled woman's house each Tuesday. I will
reckon with dirt. *bitte*, she croaks anciently, *Fenster
putzen*. work not of an angel's gate nor of the
pathway to discovery. later, receiving anomalous
temperance. one cup of water, scalding the lap,
leaps across the doors of kettles.

I couldn't have answered that question, the number not yet shown to me. the little parka in the hall restores economy, divided. to touch a divot, collect earned wages. juncture, I think. someone ought to play the heroine. no cold bleak season, just slight provision for blue answers. illumination, sustenance, quick breakfast, *die Bäckerei.* wide lane along the eye peels through, narrows upon *fog.*

I don't want to announce continuous birds but have to get up. purloin grace, I dare you, 3 sharp notes. blue ceaseless breath coiling among vines of sleep and light. wake, a muss of limpid hair transposes easily. beneath a cloth to scrub, tucking. I'm not old or wizened but someday. that elderly lady's throat, scorching *Tabak*, phlegm-crone. watching me dole. out the proper rituals for household gods. you'll see. I'm going to offer up the tint of pallid toilets after cleansing. glisten-white. the lane I tripped across to get here bends right, then left, banking the driveway.

I would like to be a little narrow with you. divided
me with my own voice when I, *Stimme.* called out
from the white. flustered, just a kid really, aren't we
all? *alte Dame,* not of my blood, complains, the
white walls are still yellow. years of smoke. she says
rag in the stove, sponge in the soup. to be at light
with a profession. I have traveled arcs and outcomes
to coalesce.

to be trampled with, eye's denial of coppice. everything sighted, never once trimmed. this blue-pike world, the firmament of morning. am coming to. you, the ochre morning gem. lent, indebted to Tuesday. clean the windows she says with fusty heat. made off with oranges, juice, dribbling variants of intermarriage. misuse, consumption.

2.

then it was Thursday afternoon. backwards birth, a
Russian lesson. another woman entirely. had seen,
she saw. small cactus on the windowsill. one act, to
pack up parcels, a squadron of little language
books. without definite articles. I want to be very
adroit for you. also, to live in many probable
Englishes. Svetlana serves Russian tea. trying it out
a little, *moya dryzuuya, kak tebya,* chewing German
bread. rousted out of bed, propped up by emotion
without the accuracy of correct grammar. I want to
till prepositions for you.

gently spoken, to say, my mouth broke, to give in.
which is one way, above the rest. the verb *lieben*.
consuming Werther's sorrow in shade under these
Kastanienbäume. rustling lakes of chestnuts. the
little nannied boy will cry out later, warm milk, his
bottle. each Tuesday, the au pair climbing stairs,
das Treppenhaus. I am going to just slide over the
threshold of an old woman's white door. I want to
smatter into puzzle pieces. for you to figure me.
mop, broom, dust, mites, clatter, dirt. the
playground as shelter, branch, but now the pouring
dark. Werther don't pull your trigger.

a world in foam light, crested also, finds reason.
wiped blue-white rag the counter, large cockroach.
dare you to live. that old lady shoves bitterly. next
year, the Euro arrives on all our doorstops. her
cackle-cream bonded envelope. pulling out DMs. I
used to dream of witches. I used to fly in dreams.
she is missing some tooth. all right. the subject to
Svetlana. *nyet kracuuvuuya.* believe me, the
nominative, now crossing the tongue. exists in all
tenses. I want to acquire verbs for you.

plenty of blue-white here to foul up rain coordinates. that *jay,* this *sparrow,* walking beams, wires. autobiographically, a place again. not asking directions in this never. never-dull. particle demons, the little boy lost in other breaches. I want to fetch a dear price. not to me, a child's worry, flax hair, fingers spindling. belonging to me, these epistles read under chestnuts. also not reading and not belonging.

the first heart of work is a lonely impulse. that child

learns his p's, q's, *Liebe.* the au pair mother, *did you*

see, my mother left the DMs on the table? I did, the

envelope, have banked, ate butter with pasta.

because the old woman could not find her wallet

this past Tuesday. I want to lose my instincts. the

little boy drafts no release. but here. but here

undone. you may not always, carrying. and where.

thrusts cleft, left-bone, wrist pushing a cart, 2

heavy cases. I speak. the time ends, little parts.

3.

defined by local time, the aeroplane descends, a
grief-note to leave. some pitch called from the
white. hotel room lampshade or 23 crumpled
tissues. you had written me stuck in secret places. I
do want to spend a night in Paris, but not by
mistake. (plane-wept, put up by Air France.)
having mentioned you previously, the red lobby,
without you. the city recasts our peppery romance.

I don't want a precise or imprecise delay. Air

France's lost hour, the Munich airport, direct light.

self, the poor tongue, to miss the next plane. believe

me, Charles de Gaulle is a maze. speaks English,

you don't tip here he says. *excuse moi, Monsieur, je*

ne parl paux ... parlez vouz? the taxi, sleek into

traffic, magazines in a pouch. later, knees to chest

then scrubbing my face. fright in the water, strange

space.

in a red alcove I slide upon a nose some glasses. to cradle the mere telephone, dialing, paltry. the white of how I have nothing white or red to sleep in. I want to call you from the white, blank white, blank, full, blue-white Bavarian sky and hear you as if I am still sitting at our bank of windows and you are in the kitchen, cutting lemons. you, whom I have been mentioning. don't pretend that when I say *who*, upon returning. is not a blank relief of tearing. some Werther-price.

or briefly, what animals, I mean the crossing. the
Atlantic, also frightening, but too low to be seen.
returning state-side to employ, no dilly-dally,
pressing up from the mattress. to answer bilious
questions, suppositions about books, *a blue cover,*
she insists, *do you know it?* I do not. pacing through
shelter.

the lining of work, that lane, once other-countried,
now here. mirror, note, liquidity, despair. in the
bathroom at home when I sobbed before my shift
because I wanted to go back to you and my mother
did not understand. leaving is worthless. what
cleaves. as Lotte, fainting, had been feared for. that
window, leaking in light. don't say coffee, a stark
word about habit sweetened with milk.

4.

this order of white, calling from white (work), years
later, cloud or tooth, eggshell (albumin), or plain
stock bonded paper (to be typed upon) or ridge of
uncut nail (French manicure) or matte surrounding
a photograph (hung above brown shelves, stacked
against the opposite wall) or whiteout (the
demarcation of error) or snow, flakes of snow
falling, snow caking a windshield—

or frost (the allocation of water, the rush to thaw in order to commence the drive to work) or a whiteboard (don't say 'conference room,' no one ever confers, here there are only directives) or chalk or a zebra's one half or chalk (a child's drawing) or whiteboard, which can so easily once again be made plain.

again I will return to you I tell this eye in the
morning. the moment dents, we do belong.
Werther, laying down his weapon, Lotte, at last,
awake. not wholly to ourselves alone, what the day
apprehends. pushing open doors after work, the
elocution of weather. the path of all the eye I have.
instances, remembrances, pale history, lists.

fractured afternoon. light hemorrhaging. I want to destruct economies for you. driving troubled children to the pool, vans long as boats. a great color, the white paint, these fuming clouds. refolded the jeans wall. extracted timelines from research, traveled cities, compiling expense reports (ate at Subway). if I save up enough destiny. if I bend you hard enough. bone-seam. everything that comes after a sequence is part of the sequence.

you *do* think of an angel's gate but I say violets.
abundant in this garden, below the stone ledge.
what I thought would be difficult turns out to be
difficult. still, what you told me. I hold up your
scrap, that you would always. could look to you in
this *fog*, those words neither droopy nor pleated.
what I thought would be difficult turns out to be
easy.

5.

bunte, you say, casting up striated paper
kites. in which I am handed, saying *now,*
meaning *is.* handed a chain of letters,
airmail, thin paper, light blue. photos and
correspondence, after you, the future before
email. when you tell me *ich komme.* still,
who is stuck, who ameliorates. *Schirre,*
cutting white away from a photograph. I
want to decide how you matter.

all right. I double-dog dare you. a strip of 4
photos, the automat, you, one leg pressed,
each accidental memory. beige curtains,
inserting DMs. who you *were* and who you
are, 2 separate species. so marked, the red
lobby boards me now. actually, not quite. I
want to explain to you about corners.

braun-äugig. 'believe me, I'll visit you.' you
also to a place, red walls, saying furrowed,
but not completely torn. besides. I was never
thinking of shopping at the mall. rather
more of cooking lessons, turning soil in the
garden. years later, at work, scrubbing
hands, just lavender soap. letting the cake
slip into the sink. squadrons of bubbles, a
whole system for lathering.

please may I declare I am not fooled. and

not. this odor, the fragrance, elegant fingers.

if you are fortune, fortune finds you. you,

living only in one form, you would die from

it. declared to you, discernable, salvaged. to

wipe clean of salt. really, the expensiveness

of the soap mostly benefits the clients.

that paper kite. you went back, *zurück*,
tumbling the airport. what I found here
doesn't pay so much at all. I form all your
transoms, then hide you in my sweater
drawer. who will write this parallel novel?
Werther soldiering through *Alltag*, the all-
day. just spills out, the impulse to eat.
Semmeln, breakfast rolls, *Wurst,* wurst,
Kaffee, coffee, *Orangensaft,* orange juice.

NOTES:

careful, body. you are full of troubled space. Werther is a youth, stunted, but Goethe himself works past it. as one would a glitch. all the sycophants in the garden can't bend towards this diligence or shake trees of fog. Werther if you walk through that glade. he says. if you stuff away that tremendous feeling for one moment like a yellow-green knit scarf pushed into a pocket. that feeling that rises again in your throat like coarse, hot bile. the story, supposedly about us here in our movements. the body feeling rather weak.

somehow, someone notes it down. conversing with the great man, 1829. *we talked about the Theory of Colors; and among other things about drinking glasses.* imbibing from tall, fluted stances. I needn't explain to you about light on the glasses. how phenomena is perceived. to bridge a body and a mind. when I first began the parallel novel, the orange juice was so delicious and sweet I tasted the bright orange color. really. once the great man. storm in his chest. if Werther had just understood about the colors and the drinking glasses.

Werther tore pages to read a line. later, the great man, in his dotage, conducts experiments. light and shadow. in our own eyes, it's true. well, he got us here. *Lotte is a feeling without comparison ... a neighbor saw the flash of the powder and heard the shot, but as everything was quiet afterwards, paid no further attention ... about eleven in the evening he* [Werther] *was taken to the grave ... craftsman carried him ... no priests accompanied him.* Werther is an emotion without the violet heat of sense. Goethe, the great man, massages past-marbles. can see extinguished portents in the colored glass. he had come very close. passion writes us a permission slip to survive it.

Acknowledgments

Many thanks to all at Black Lawrence Press for their dedication in seeing this project through from its original manuscript form to published chapbook.

Additional thanks to the editors at Horse Less Press for publishing the Notes sections online in *Horse Less Review*.

And finally, thanks to Steven Meredith, without whose steadfast friendship and unflagging support I wouldn't be where I am today, and to whom this series of poems is dedicated, not because they are about him, but because the heart, heat, and sense of exploration that I gain from our life together infuse everything I write.

Photo: Steven Meredith

Jenny Drai studied German language and literature as an undergraduate, after which she lived in Munich for several years, working various odd jobs, including au pair, English tutor, and cleaning woman. After her return to the United States, she obtained an MFA in Poetry from Saint Mary's College of California. She is the author of *Letters to Quince* (winner of the Deerbird Novella Prize from Artistically Declined Press, 2015) and a full-length collection of poetry, *[the door]*, (Trembling Pilllow Press, 2015). Another chapbook, *: Body Wolf :,* appeared recently from Horse Less Press. Her poetry has appeared in numerous online and print journals, including *American Letters & Commentary*, *New American Writing*, the *Volta*, *Handsome*, and *Jellyfish*. She is currently at work on a novel. You can find her at jennydraiisferal.tumblr.com and @jenny_drai.